Ears Are For Hearing

by Paul Showers   illustrated by Holly Keller

Thomas Y. Crowell   New York

The *Let's-Read-and-Find-Out Science Book* series was originated by Dr. Franklyn M. Branley, Astronomer Emeritus and former Chairman of the American Museum-Hayden Planetarium, and was formerly co-edited by him and Dr. Roma Gans, Professor Emeritus of Childhood Education, Teachers College, Columbia University. For a complete catalog of Let's-Read-and-Find-Out Science Books, write to Thomas Y. Crowell Junior Books, Harper & Row, Publishers, Inc., 10 East 53rd Street, New York, NY 10022.

Library of Congress Cataloging-in-Publication Data
Showers, Paul.
   Ears are for hearing / by Paul Showers ; illustrated by Holly Keller.
      p.   cm. — (Let's-read-and-find-out science book)
   Summary: Describes the process of hearing, during which sound waves travel through the ear and become signals the brain interprets as individual sounds.
   ISBN 0-690-04718-5 : $. — ISBN 0-690-04720-7 (lib. bdg.) : $
   1. Hearing—Juvenile literature. 2. Ear—Juvenile literature.
[1. Hearing. 2. Ear.] I. Keller, Holly, ill. II. Title.
III. Series.
QP462.2.S56 1990   89-17479
612.8'5—dc20   CIP
                                                          AC

Ears Are For Hearing

Put your hands behind your ears. Bend your ears
forward. Take your hands away. Do it again: ears forward,
hands away. Do it several times. Can you hear the
difference? Your ears collect sounds. They collect a little
more sound when your hands help them.

Sound travels through the air in waves. There are thousands and thousands of different sound waves. Sound waves are made by a guitar, by a plane up in the sky, by a fire truck, by people talking. You cannot see these sound waves. But you can hear them with your ears. This is how you do it.

You cannot see all of your ear. You see only the outside part. This part is called the outer ear. The rest of your ear is safe inside your head. It is inside the hard bones of your skull.

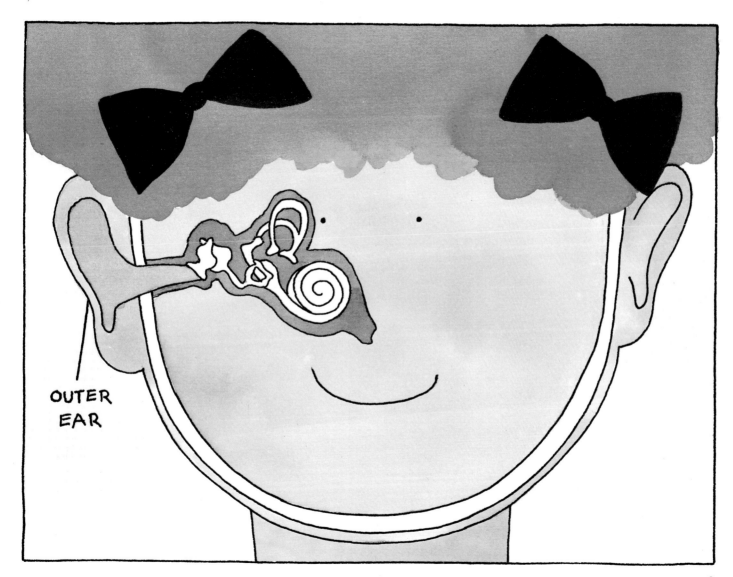

OUTER
EAR

The outer ear is like a cup. It collects the sound waves in the air around your head. There is a hole near the bottom of the cup. Sound waves push through the hole into a little tunnel. The tunnel is called the auditory canal. The end of the auditory canal is closed off by a membrane, which is something like a layer of thin skin. This membrane is called the eardrum.

On the other side of the eardrum is the middle ear.

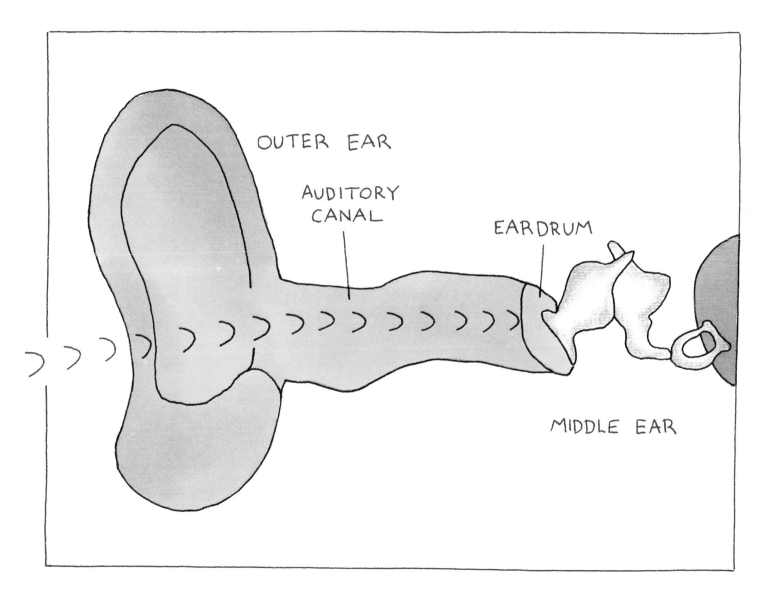

OUTER EAR

AUDITORY CANAL

EARDRUM

MIDDLE EAR

11

The middle ear is like a little room. The eardrum is at one end of the room. At the other end is a small opening called the oval window. It is covered by a membrane, too. Between the eardrum and the oval window are three tiny bones. They are called the hammer, the anvil, and the stirrup, because they look a little like a real hammer, anvil, and stirrup.

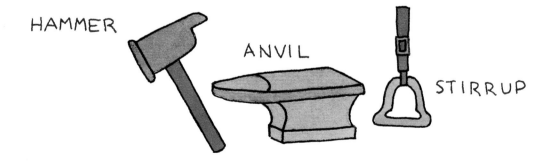

HAMMER   ANVIL   STIRRUP

The tiny bones are fastened together. They stretch across the middle ear like a chain. The hammer is at one end of the chain. It is fastened to the eardrum. Next comes the anvil, then the stirrup. The flat part of the stirrup fits against the membrane of the oval window.

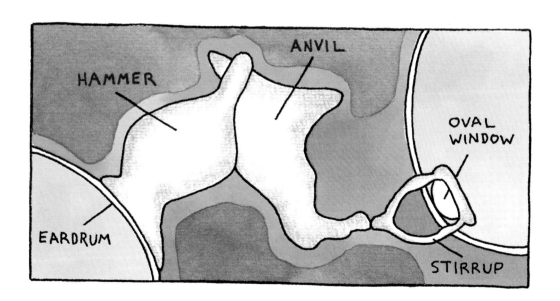

On the other side of the oval window is the inner ear. It has several parts. The part next to the oval window is called the vestibule. It opens into a tiny tube that is curled up like a snail shell. This curled part is called the cochlea. The vestibule and the cochlea are filled with fluid.

Inside the cochlea is the part of the ear you actually hear with. It is called the organ of Corti. It was named for the man who first studied it under a microscope. His name was Alfonso Corti.

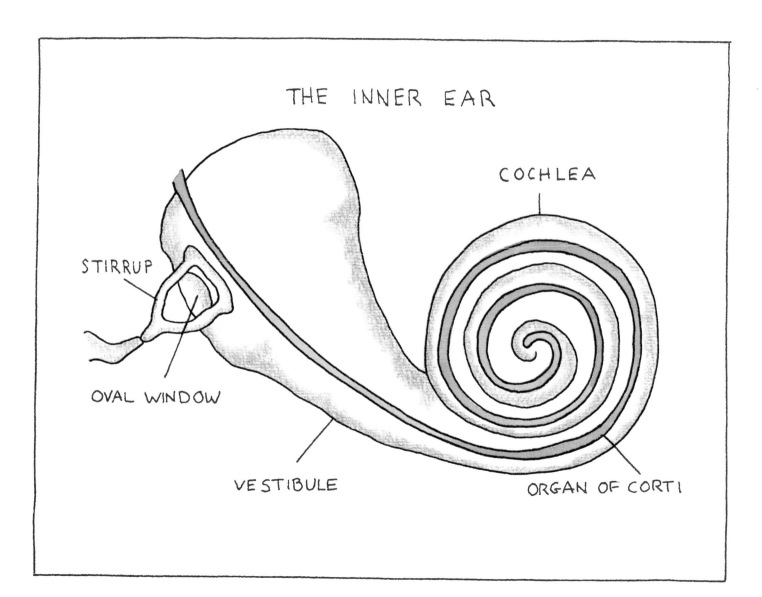

THE INNER EAR

COCHLEA

STIRRUP

OVAL WINDOW

VESTIBULE

ORGAN OF CORTI

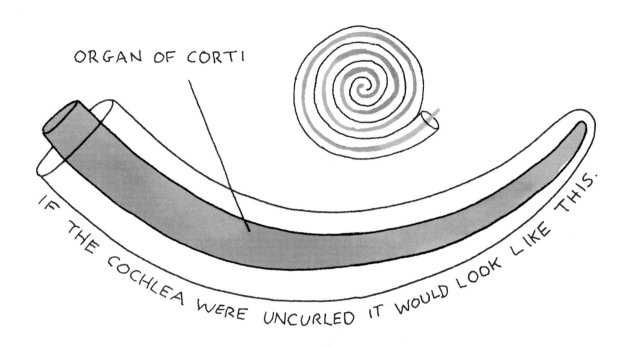

ORGAN OF CORTI

IF THE COCHLEA WERE UNCURLED IT WOULD LOOK LIKE THIS.

The organ of Corti is stretched out inside the cochlea like a long, narrow ribbon. It is made up of thousands of special hearing cells. Each hearing cell has tiny hairs on it. These hairs are called cilia.

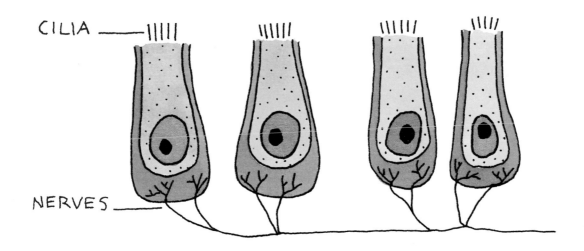

CILIA

NERVES

Each hearing cell is connected to a threadlike nerve. The nerves carry signals the way telephone wires carry sounds. This is how it all works.

Sound waves in the air pour into the auditory canal. They bump against the eardrum and shake it back and forth. When the eardrum shakes, it shakes the hammer. Then the anvil and the stirrup begin to shake. When the stirrup shakes against the membrane of the oval window, it starts up waves in the fluid of the vestibule and the cochlea.

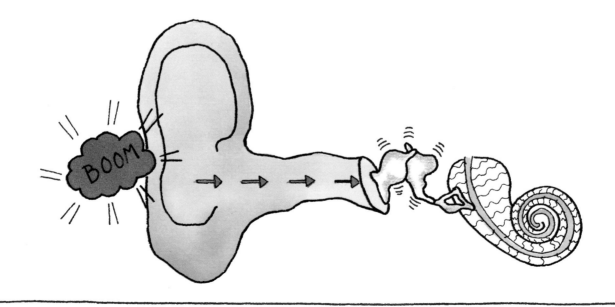

As the waves pass through the fluid of the cochlea, the cilia of the special hearing cells bend the way grass bends when a breeze blows over it. When the cilia bend, the hearing cells begin to send out signals. The nerves connected to them pass the signals up to your brain.

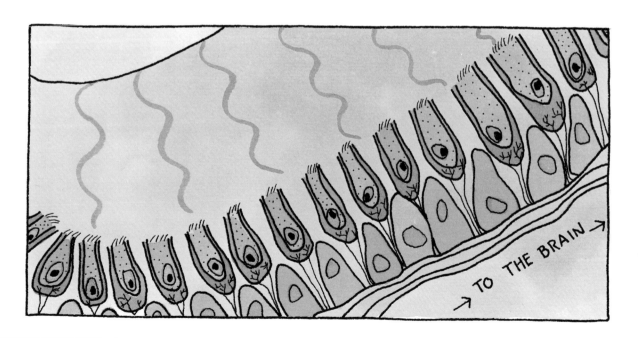

Your brain receives the signals and makes sense out of them. It can tell the signals of an airplane from the signals of a guitar. It can pay attention to the TV and a fire truck out in the street and to your mother talking to you—all at the same time. It hardly ever gets the signals mixed up.

Your inner ear helps you to hear. It also helps you to keep your balance. Just above the vestibule are three small curved tubes. They are called the semicircular canals. They are filled with their own fluid, and they have their own special cells to send out signals.

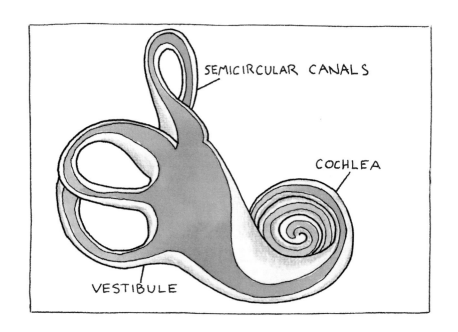

SEMICIRCULAR CANALS

COCHLEA

VESTIBULE

When you turn around, or lie down, or stand on your head, or make any other movement, the fluid moves around in the semicircular canals. It presses on the special cells. These cells send signals through their own nerves to your brain. Then your brain sends signals to your muscles to hold steady. This all happens quicker than a wink.

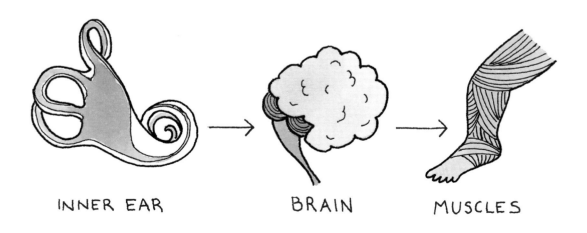

INNER EAR   BRAIN   MUSCLES

It takes your muscles time to learn how to hold steady. It takes practice to train them so that you keep your balance while walking or roller-skating, or doing a cartwheel. But your inner ear and your brain never need practice. They work together so well that you never even think about it.

Your inner ear is safe inside your head, but even there it can be hurt. Very loud sounds that last too long will harm it. When very loud sounds crash into your outer ear, they make strong waves in the fluid of your inner ear. The strong waves press the cilia down flat. If the waves last too long or happen too often, some of the cilia get hurt. They can't bend back up. The hearing cells can't send out signals to your brain. Then you become deaf to certain sounds.

DAMAGED CILIA

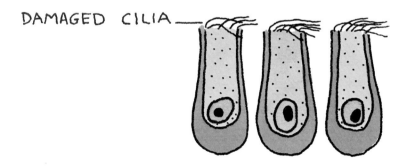

Loud sounds are bad for your inner ear. Here are some rules to remember. Don't stand too close to a jackhammer. Don't turn your stereo up as loud as you can make it. If any sound hurts your ears—like the screech of a police-car siren or a fire engine passing by—don't be embarrassed to put your hands over your ears.

Take care of your wonderful inner ear. You'll never get a new one.